# KIDS ON EARTH

*Wildlife Adventures – Explore The World*
*Kingfisher - Madagascar*

Sensei Paul David

# COPYRIGHT PAGE

Kids On Earth: Wildlife Adventures - Explore The World

Kingfisher - Madagascar

by Sensei Paul David,

Copyright © 2023.

All rights reserved.

978-1-77848-173-4 KoE_WildLife_Amazon_PaperbackBook_madagascar_kingfisher

978-1-77848-172-7 KoE_WildLife_Amazon_eBook_madagascar_kingfisher

978-1-77848-417-9 KoE_Wildlife_Ingram_Paperbackbook_KingFisherBird

This book is not authorized for free distribution copying.

www.senseipublishing.com

@senseipublishing
#senseipublishing

## Synopsis

Fun Facts about the Kingfisher in Madagascar is an entertaining and informative book for children aged 6 to 12. It provides an overview of the colorful bird and its unique behavior, as well as its importance to the island's ecosystem. Through 30 unique fun facts, children will learn everything they need to know about the Kingfisher in Madagascar, from its diet to its habitat and its significance in local culture. With its vivid illustrations and easy-to-understand language, this book is sure to be a hit with young readers!

# Get Our FREE Books Now!

kidsonearth.life

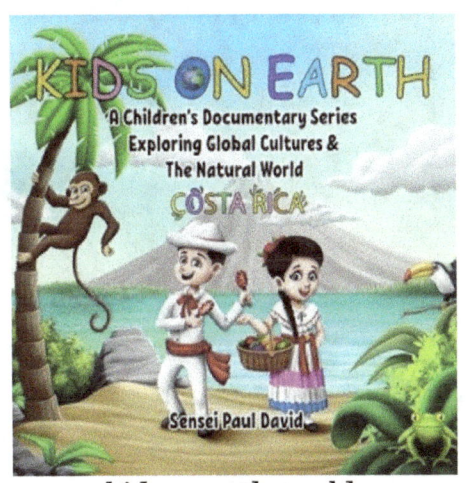

kidsonearth.world

# Click Below for Another Book In Each Series

senseipublishing.com/KoE_SERIES

senseipublishing.com/KoE_Wildlife_SERIES

## KoE En Español

senseipublishing.com/KoE_SERIES_SPANISH

www.senseipublishing.com

# Join Our Publishing Journey!

If you would like to receive FUTURE FREE BOOKS and get to know us better, please click www.senseipublishing.com and join our newsletter by entering your email address in the pop-up box.

**Follow Our Blog: senseipauldavid.ca**

Follow/Like/Subscribe: Facebook, Instagram, YouTube: @senseipublishing

Scan the QR Code with your phone or tablet to follow us on social media:

Like / Subscribe / Follow

## Introduction

Welcome to Fun Facts about the Kingfisher in Madagascar! In this book, you'll learn everything you need to know about this fascinating bird. Kingfishers are known for their unique behavior, colorful plumage, and swift flight. From its diet to its habitat, you'll discover everything you need to know about the Kingfisher in Madagascar. So, let's get started!

The Kingfisher is a colorful bird native to Madagascar. Its bright blue feathers are a striking contrast against the lush greenery of the island.

Kingfishers feed primarily on small fish, as well as other aquatic creatures such as amphibians, insects, and crustaceans.

Kingfishers use their beaks to catch prey by diving into the water from a perch.

Kingfishers are very territorial and often fight to protect their territory.

Kingfishers have very loud calls that can be heard from a great distance.

Kingfishers mate for life, and they will often stay in the same area for an entire breeding season.

Kingfishers can be found in both freshwater and saltwater habitats.

Kingfishers have an impressive wingspan of up to two feet.

Kingfishers have a very distinctive flight pattern, which involves zig-zagging and swooping.

The Kingfisher is a diurnal bird, meaning it is active during the day.

Kingfishers build nests in tree hollows or on cliffs.

Kingfishers are monogamous, and they typically mate for life.

Kingfishers lay their eggs in shallow water.

Kingfishers are often seen perched on branches near water, waiting for prey.

Kingfishers typically live in small family groups, with one breeding pair and their offspring.

Kingfishers can live up to 10 years in the wild.

The Kingfisher is a stunningly beautiful bird, with bright blue feathers and a red beak.

Kingfishers are very vocal birds, and their calls can often be heard echoing through the forests of Madagascar.

Kingfishers are expert fishermen, and they can catch prey up to 10 times their body weight.

Kingfishers hunt by plunging into the water and grabbing prey with their beaks.

Kingfishers are very fast fliers, and they can reach speeds of up to 60 miles per hour.

Kingfishers migrate to Madagascar during the summer months, and they return to Africa during the winter.

Kingfishers are sensitive to environmental changes and can be affected by deforestation and other human activities.

Kingfishers are protected by the Convention on International Trade in Endangered Species of Wild Fauna and Flora (CITES).

Kingfishers are a vital part of the ecosystem, as they help keep insect and fish populations in balance.

51

Kingfishers have many predators, including snakes, cats, and other birds of prey.

Kingfishers have a special adaptation that allows them to see in both air and water.

Kingfishers use their beaks to dig burrows into the mud or sand.

The Kingfisher has a very unique and recognizable call that is used to warn others of potential danger.

The Kingfisher is an important part of the island's culture and is celebrated in many traditional songs and stories.

61

## Conclusion

We hope you've enjoyed learning about the Kingfisher in Madagascar! From its diet to its habitat, you've discovered a lot about this amazing bird. You've also learned about its importance to the island's ecosystem and its significance in the local culture. With its bright blue feathers and loud calls, the Kingfisher is truly a unique bird.

# Thank you for reading this book!

If you found this book helpful, I would be grateful if you would **post an honest review on Amazon** so this book can reach other supportive readers like you!

All you need to do is digitally flip to the back and leave your review. Or visit amazon.com/author/senseipauldavid click the correct book cover and click on the blue link next to the yellow stars that say, "customer reviews."

*As always...*

*It's a great day to be alive!*

## Share Our FREE eBooks Now!

kidsonearth.life

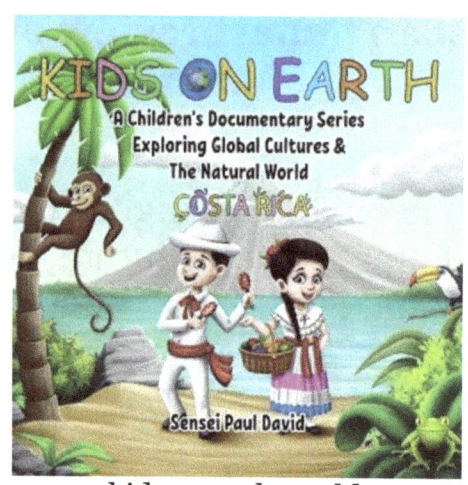

kidsonearth.world

# Click Below for Another Book In Each Series

senseipublishing.com/KoE_SERIES

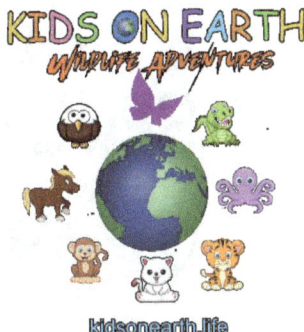

senseipublishing.com/KoE_Wildlife_SERIES

## KoE En Español

senseipublishing.com/KoE_SERIES_SPANISH

www.senseipublishing.com

www.senseipublishing.com

@senseipublishing
#senseipublishing

Check out our **recommendations** for other books for adults & kids plus other great resources by visiting
www.senseipublishing.com/resources/

# Join Our Publishing Journey!

If you would like to receive FREE BOOKS and special offers, please visit www.senseipublishing.com and join our newsletter by entering your email address in the pop-up box

## Follow Our Engaging Blog NOW!
## senseipauldavid.ca

## Get Our FREE Books Today!

Click & Share the Links Below

### FREE Kids Books
lifeofbailey.senseipublishing.com
kidsonearth.senseipublishing.com

### FREE Self-Development Book

senseiselfdevelopment.senseipublishing.com

**FREE BONUS!!!**
**Experience Over 25 FREE Engaging Guided Meditations!**

Prized Skills & Practices for Adults & Kids. Help Restore Deep Sleep, Lower Stress, Improve Posture, Navigate Uncertainty & More.

Download the Free Insight Timer App and click the link below:
**http://insig.ht/sensei_paul**

# About Sensei Publishing

Sensei Publishing commits itself to helping people of all ages transform into better versions of themselves by providing high-quality and research-based self-development books with an emphasis on mental health and guided meditations. Sensei Publishing offers well-written e-books, audiobooks, paperbacks, and online courses that simplify complicated but practical topics in line with its mission to inspire people toward positive transformation.

It's a great day to be alive!

# About the Author

I create simple & transformative eBooks & Guided Meditations for Adults & Children proven to help navigate uncertainty, solve niche problems & bring families closer together.

I'm a former finance project manager, private pilot, jiu-jitsu instructor, musician & former University of Toronto Fitness Trainer. I prefer a science-based approach to focus on these & other areas in my life to stay humble & hungry to evolve. I hope you enjoy my work and I'd love to hear your feedback.

- It's a great day to be alive!
Sensei Paul David

Scan & Follow/Like/Subscribe: Facebook, Instagram, YouTube: @senseipublishing

Scan using your phone/iPad camera for Social Media
Visit us at www.senseipublishing.com and sign up for our newsletter to learn more about our exciting books and to experience our FREE Guided Meditations for Kids & Adults.

www.ingramcontent.com/pod-product-compliance
Lightning Source LLC
Chambersburg PA
CBHW080616110526
44587CB00040BB/3728